FACTS ABOUT THE MOON

OTHER BOOKS BY DORIANNE LAUX

Awake

What We Carry

Smoke

*The Poet's Companion: A Guide to
the Pleasures of Writing Poetry*
(with Kim Addonizio)

FACTS ABOUT THE MOON

POEMS

Dorianne Laux

W. W. NORTON & COMPANY   NEW YORK LONDON

Excerpt from "The Moon at Zenith" from *The Complete Poems of Anna
Akhmatova,* translated by Judith Hemschemeyer, edited and introduced
by Roberta Reeder. Copyright © 1989, 1992, 1997 by Judith Hemschemeyer.
Reprinted by permission of Zephyr Press.

For information about permission to reproduce selections from this book,
write to Permissions, W. W. Norton & Company, Inc.,
500 Fifth Avenue, New York, NY 101110

Manufacturing by Courier Westford
Book design by Anna Oler

Library of Congress Cataloging-in-Publication Data

Laux, Dorianne.
Facts about the moon : poems / Dorianne Laux.—1st ed.
p. cm.
ISBN 0-393-06096-9
1. Women—poetry. 2. Working class—poetry. I. Title.
PS3562.A8455F33   2005
811'.54—dc22   2005024079

W. W. Norton & Company, Inc.
500 Fifth Avenue, New York, N.Y. 10110
www.wwnorton.com

W. W. Norton & Company Ltd.
Castle House, 75/76 Wells Street, London W1T 3QT

1 2 3 4 5 6 7 8 9 0

FOR JOE
AND OUR STARLING COLETTE

Who would dare tell me that
I am a stranger here?!?

—Anna Akhmatova,
"The Moon at Zenith"

✳

CONTENTS

*

****

FACTS ABOUT THE MOON

THE LIFE OF TREES

The pines rub their great noise
into the spangled dark, scratch
their itchy boughs against the house,
and that moan's mystery translates roughly
into drudgery of ownership: time
to drag the ladder from the shed,
climb onto the roof with a saw
between my teeth, cut
those suckers down. What's reality
if not a long exhaustive cringe
from the blade, the teeth? I want to sleep
and dream the life of trees, beings
from the muted world who care
nothing for Money, Politics, Power,
Will or Right, who want little from the night
but a few dead stars going dim, a white owl
lifting from their limbs, who want only
to sink their roots into the wet ground
and terrify the worms or shake
their bleary heads like fashion models
or old hippies. If trees could speak
they wouldn't, only hum some low
green note, roll their pinecones
down the empty streets and blame it,

with a shrug, on the cold wind.
During the day they sleep inside
their furry bark, clouds shredding
like ancient lace above their crowns.
Sun. Rain. Snow. Wind. They fear
nothing but the Hurricane, and Fire,
that whipped bully who rises up
and becomes his own dead father.
In the storms the young ones
bend and bend and the old know
they may not make it, go down
with the power lines sparking,
broken at the trunk. They fling
their branches, forked sacrifice
to the beaten earth. They do not pray.
If they make a sound it's eaten
by the wind. And though the stars
return they do not offer thanks, only
ooze a thicker sap from their roundish
concentric wounds, clap the water
from their needles, straighten their spines
and breathe, and breathe again.

DEMOCRACY

When you're cold—November, the streets icy and everyone
    you pass
homeless, Goodwill coats and Hefty bags torn up to make
    ponchos—
someone is always at the pay phone, hunched over the receiver

spewing winter's germs, swollen lipped, face chapped, making
    the last
tired connection of the day. You keep walking to keep the cold
at bay, too cold to wait for the bus, too depressing the thought

of entering that blue light, the chilled eyes watching you decide
which seat to take: the man with one leg, his crutches bumping
the smudged window glass, the woman with her purse clutched

to her breasts like a dead child, the boy, pimpled, morose, his
    head
shorn, a swastika carved into the stubble, staring you down.
So you walk into the cold you know: the wind, indifferent
    blade,

familiar, the gold leaves heaped along the gutters. You have
a home, a house with gas heat, a toilet that flushes. You have
a credit card, cash. You could take a taxi if one would show up.

You can feel it now: why people become Republicans: *Get
that dog*
*off the street. Remove that spit and graffiti. Arrest those people
huddled*
on the steps of the church. If it weren't for them you could
believe in god,

in freedom, the bus would appear and open its doors, the
driver dressed
in his tan uniform, pants legs creased, dapper hat: *Hello Miss,
watch*
your step now. But you're not a Republican. You're only tired,
hungry,

you want out of the cold. So you give up, walk back, step into
line behind
the grubby vet who hides a bag of wine under his pea coat,
holds out
his grimy 85 cents, takes each step slow as he pleases, releases
his coins

into the box and waits as they chink down the chute, stakes
out a seat
in the back and eases his body into the stained vinyl to dream
as the chips of shrapnel in his knee warm up and his good leg

flops into the aisle. And you'll doze off, too, in a while, next to
    the girl
who can't sit still, who listens to her Walkman and taps her
    boots
to a rhythm you can't hear, but you can see it—when she bops

her head and her hands do a jive in the air—you can feel it
as the bus rolls on, stopping at each red light in a long wheeze,
jerking and idling, rumbling up and lurching off again.

VACATION SEX

We've been at it all summer, from the Canadian border
to the edge of Mexico, just barely keeping it American
but doing okay just the same, in hotels under overpasses
or rooms next to ice machines, friends' fold-out couches,
in-laws' guest quarters—wallpaper and bedspreads festooned
with nautical rigging, tiny life rings and coiled tow ropes—

even one night in the car, the plush backseat not plush
enough, the door handle giving me an impromptu
sacro-cranial chiropractic adjustment, the underside
of the front seat strafing the perfect arches of his feet.
And one long glorious night in a cabin tucked in the woods
where our crooning and whooping started the coyotes

singing. But the best was when we got home, our luggage
cuddled in the vestibule—really just a hallway
but because we were home it seemed like a vestibule—
and we threw off our vestments, which were really
just our clothes but they seemed like garments, like raiment,
like habits because we felt sorely religious, dropping them

one by one on the stairs: white shirts, black bra, blue jeans,
red socks, then stood naked in our own bedroom, our bed
with its drab spread, our pillows that smelled like us:

a little shampoo-y, maybe a little like myrrh, the gooseberry
candle we light sometimes when we're in the mood for mood,
our own music and books and cap off the toothpaste and cat

on the window seat. Our window looks over a parking lot—
a dental group—and at night we can hear the cars whisper past
the 24-hour Albertson's where the homeless couple
buys their bag of wine before they walk across the street
to sit on the dentist's bench under a tree and swap it
and guzzle it and argue loudly until we all fall asleep.

THE RAVENS OF DENALI

Such dumb luck. To stumble
across an "unkindness" of ravens
at play with a shred of clear visquine
fallen from the blown-out window
of the Denali Truck Stop and Café.
Black wings gathering in the deserted
parking lot below the Assembly of God.
Ravens at play in the desolate fields
of the lord, under the tallest mountain
in North America, eight of them,
as many as the stars in the Big Dipper
on Alaska's state flag, yellow stars
sewn to a blue background flapping
from a pole over the roadside.
Flag that Benny Benson, age 13,
an Alutiiq Indian of Seward
formerly housed at the Jesse-Lee Memorial
Home for Orphans in Unalaska,
designed and submitted to a contest
in 1927 and won, his crayoned masterpiece
snapping above every broken-down
courthouse, chipped brick library
and deathtrap post office
in the penultimate state accepted

to the Union, known to its people
as the Upper One. Though a design
of the northern lights would have been
my choice, those alien green curtains
swirling over Mt. McKinley, Denali,
"the tall one," during the coldest, darkest
months of the subarctic year.
Red starburst or purple-edged skirt
rolling in vitreous waves
over the stunted ice-rimed treetops
or in spring, candles of fireweed
and the tiny ice blue flowers
of the tundra. Tundra, a word
that sounds like a thousand caribou
pouring down a gorge.
But all that might be difficult
for an orphaned 7th grader to draw
with three chewed-up crayons
and a piece of butcher paper.
As would these eight giggling ravens
with their shrewd eyes and silt-shine wings,
beaks like keloid scars. Acrobats
of speed and sheen. Black boot
of the bird family. Unconcerned

this moment with survival.
Though I hope they survive.
Whatever we have in store for them.
And the grizzly bear and the club-
footed moose. The muscular salmon.
The oil-spill seal and gull.
And raven's cousin, the bald eagle,
who can dive at 100 miles per hour,
can actually swim with massive
butterfly strokes through
the great glacial lakes of Alaska,
her wingspan as long as a man.
Architect of the two-ton nest
assembled over 34 years
with scavenged branches,
threatened in all but three
of the Lower 48, but making, by god,
a comeback if it's not too late
for such lofty promises.
Even the homely marmot
and the immigrant starling,
I wish you luck,
whatever ultimate harm we do
to this northernmost up-flung arm

of our country, our revolving world.
But you, epicurean raven, may you
be the pole star of the apocalypse,
you stubborn snow trudger,
you quorum of eight who jostle one another
for a strip of plastic on the last
endless day, the last endless night
of our only sun's solar wind,
those glorious auroras, glassine gowns
of Blake's angels, that almost invisible shine
tugged and stretched between you
like taffy from outer space, tattered ends
gripped in your fur-crested beaks as we reel
headlong into the dwindling unknown.
Denizens of the frozen north, the last
frontier, harbingers of unluck
and the cold bleak lack to come.

THE CROSSING

The elk of Orick wait patiently to cross the road
and my husband of six months, who thinks

he's St. Francis, climbs out of the car to assist.
Ghost of St. Francis, his T-shirt flapping, steps

tenderly onto the tarmac and they begin their trek,
heads lifted, nostrils flared, each footfall

a testament to stalled momentum, gracefully
hesitant, as a brace of semis, lined up, humming,

adjust their air brakes. They cross the four-lane
like a coronation, slow as a Greek frieze, river

wind riffling the wheat grass of their rumps.
But my husband stays on, to talk to the one

who won't budge, oblivious to her sisters,
a long stalk of fennel gyrating between her teeth.

Go on, he beseeches, *Get going*, but the lone elk
stands her ground, their noses less than a yard apart.

One stubborn creature staring down another.
This is how I know the marriage will last.

HUMMINGBIRD

We buried the hummingbird
in his mantle of light, buried
him deep in the loam, one eye
staring into the earth's fiery
core, the other up through
the door in the sky. His needle
beak pointed east, his curled
feet west, and we each touched
our fingertips to his breast
before lifting them up from
the darkness to kiss. And
from our blessed fists we
rained the powdery dirt
down, erasing the folded
wings, the dream-colored
head, tamping the torn grass
with the heels of our hands,
our bare feet, summer almost
over, swaying together on the great
ship of death as clouds sailed by,
blowing our hair and the wind
walked us back to our room.

MY BROTHER'S GRAVE

I flew from Oregon to Maine in 1995
to see the town I was taken from
when I was two, the street, the shuttered
house my parents lived in. I stayed
with a family on a farm, fell in love
with the husband and wife, wanted
to enter them like water, become
their lover, and when I saw
that was impossible, become their child.
They already had three children
so what could I do but wander the roads
drinking coffee from a paper cup,
eating a day-old baguette, visit
the mill where my father worked,
making cards and envelopes, his hand
on an iron lever. I tried to see
through the scarred windows
of the two-room bungalow, touched
the numbers hanging from nails by the door.
In the middle of Water Street Bridge
I leaned over the railing holding
onto a black umbrella, dug out
a pebble wedged in the latticework
and threw it into the river.

I walked back to the town hall
and asked for a map of the graveyard
where my brother lay all these sad years,
his sweet face and long legs
buried under the dirt, and the lady
behind the counter was nice to me,
looked up at the little bell that tinked
when I stepped in saying *comment ça va?*
then drew a crooked line down the paths
with a blue Magic Marker, making
a little star over his name. I stopped
at the flower shop, of course
they had a flower shop, but decided
against and kept walking, pulling up
weeds from the roadside, some coming out
by the roots, tough, stringy stems
I had to chew off with my teeth,
the pitiful blossoms sodden, barely there.
It was a small sunken city, a light
summer rain, a narrow path, but
I found him, finally, and sat down,
my paper cup full of the pale yellow
weeds of Maine: loosestrife, clover,
dodder, common cinquefoil.

When I set them on the slight mound
they toppled over on the grass where
they looked like old bruises. To say I cried
would not do justice to the moment.
To say I felt my brother's presence
would be a lie. He was my brother.
I hardly knew him. He was there one day
then he was dust. I was twelve.
What did I know?
How could I have imagined then
how alone I would become.

THE LAST DAYS OF POMPEII

What if the ashes came down on us,
a black avalanche trapping our bodies
in their twenty-first century beds,
your spine buttressed with pillows,
wearing taped-up wire glasses,
an old book cracked open
against the knobs of your knees.
And me curled next to you, one hand
on your chest like a wind-blown
blossom, in socks and T-shirt, asleep,
just beginning to dream.

Preserved for time without end
this end-of-day tableau, on view
in a glass room in the future's
museum, two dragonflies sealed
in amber or ice. Or ruined statues,
arms and heads lopped off,
the painstaking calculations
of geometry and physics, reconstructing,
from whorled stumps, our inner lives:

the possum bent on a wet road in the blue
headlights of my dream, the marriage

of our bodies only moments before
the ash rushed in like the sea, sheathing
each small thing in cinders and shadows,
what we gave each other encased
in dust: the ring on the sink, a brass angel
with hammered wings, their meaning
a secret even from us, your eyes
seared blind for eternity, my hair
splayed against pillows of dirt
like a handful of dark straw.

MOON IN THE WINDOW

I wish I could say I was the kind of child
who watched the moon from her window,
would turn toward it and wonder.
I never wondered. I read. Dark signs
that crawled toward the edge of the page.
It took me years to grow a heart
from paper and glue. All I had
was a flashlight, bright as the moon,
a white hole blazing beneath the sheets.

FACTS ABOUT THE MOON

The moon is backing away from us
an inch and a half each year. That means
if you're like me and were born
around fifty years ago the moon
was a full six feet closer to the earth.
What's a person supposed to do?
I feel the gray cloud of consternation
travel across my face. I begin thinking
about the moon-lit past, how if you go back
far enough you can imagine the breathtaking
hugeness of the moon, prehistoric
solar eclipses when the moon covered the sun
so completely there was no corona, only
a darkness we had no word for.
And future eclipses will look like this: the moon
a small black pupil in the eye of the sun.
But these are bald facts.
What bothers me most is that someday
the moon will spiral right out of orbit
and all land-based life will die.
The moon keeps the oceans from swallowing
the shores, keeps the electromagnetic fields
in check at the polar ends of the earth.
And please don't tell me

what I already know, that it won't happen
for a long time. I don't care. I'm afraid
of what will happen to the moon.
Forget us. We don't deserve the moon.
Maybe we once did but not now
after all we've done. These nights
I harbor a secret pity for the moon, rolling
around alone in space without
her milky planet, her only love, a mother
who's lost a child, a bad child,
a greedy child or maybe a grown boy
who's murdered and raped, a mother
can't help it, she loves that boy
anyway, and in spite of herself
she misses him, and if you sit beside her
on the padded hospital bench
outside the door to his room you can't not
take her hand, listen to her while she
weeps, telling you how sweet he was,
how blue his eyes, and you know she's only
romanticizing, that she's conveniently
forgotten the bruises and booze,
the stolen car, the day he ripped
the phones from the walls, and you want

to slap her back to sanity, remind her
of the truth: he was a leech, a fuckup,
a little shit, and you almost do
until she lifts her pale puffy face, her eyes
two craters, and then you can't help it
either, you know love when you see it,
you can feel its lunar strength, its brutal pull.

WHAT'S BROKEN

The slate black sky. The middle step
of the back porch. And long ago

my mother's necklace, the beads
rolling north and south. Broken

the rose stem, water into drops, glass
knob on the bedroom door. Last summer's

pot of parsley and mint, white roots
shooting like streamers through the cracks.

Years ago the cat's tail, the bird bath,
the car hood's rusted latch. Broken

little finger on my right hand at birth—
I was pulled out too fast. What hasn't

been rent, divided, split? Broken
the days into nights, the night sky

into stars, the stars into patterns
I make up as I trace them

with a broken-off blade
of grass. Possible, unthinkable,

the cricket's tiny back as I lie
on the lawn in the dark, my heart

a blue cup fallen from someone's hands.

HER FIRST

Who remembers when she told me.
The year. What actually happened.
Which hospital. My mother. The man
who died in her arms. Gone from memory.
Only that he was her first. Only my mother
in her uniform, white, unblemished
or stippled with blood. And his eyes.
The hand she held as he held on.
Long enough to say the wordless thing
that needed saying. Her eyes answering,
then speaking aloud the only words
that could be said: *It's alright, I'm here,*
Okay. Her telling me how she held on,
never looked away, ushered his soul
into the unknown with a handful
of words, a direct gaze, almost visible,
almost a color, a cone of warmer air
shimmering between them in the bleach-
scented room, a thin stream of Muzak
blushing through the speakers
in the hallway outside the open door,
the slick canted floor they would
gurney him down on tiny rubber wheels,
that oiled, spun freely, easily,

as they turned the corner
toward the morgue, the institutional
gray walls not, thank god, the last color
he would see but the sea-blue corona
of her eyes, irises spiked with amber,
flecked with green. Fully open
and seeing him. Whoever he was.
Whoever he had harmed or helped,
loved or failed to love, finally, mercifully,
of no importance now as she watched over
the last minutes of his anonymous life.
His large death fluttering down
under the soft black wings of his lashes
as he left this sweet, brief world
and entered into the next, hand
in hand with a godless woman
who would always remember him.
His rust-colored eyes saying
good-bye to her, to this life, in a time
I remember now.

THE GERMANS

Marzipan. Blue delft cups.
Hand-carved wooden ornaments.
"O Tannenbaum." The Dittmans
were German, that hated race,
and I was too young to be under the covers
reading stories of the Holocaust.
I looked deep into their gray eyes, watched
their ruddy cheeks rise in greeting
over the redwood fence, Elizabeth
and Fred, their twin daughters,
and in my head the bodies falling,
ditches of death, crows, dogs,
their yellow teeth bared,
while in the calm backyard their schnauzer
splashed in the pool, my sisters and I
safe there, Fred lifting us up
under our bone-thin shoulders
and dunking us, his meaty hands
rough as the bricks he laid
day after day, mortar and gravel,
gritty sand thick under his fingernails.
He never once touched us in that
bad way, arms around our waists
he twirled us until the sky swam

into the grass, the roof collapsed
onto the patio, their long windows blurs
of plummeting light. He loved us.
I believe this. Or not just us,
but all children, the dog, birds,
piano music, stinky cheese, his wife's
wide back, the curled blonde hairs
at the nape of her neck.
And I had to make myself forget
the other women with their shaved heads
and caved-in chests, the men
who did not love them, that opposite of love
I never wanted to know, an iron gate opened
that could never be closed, the uniformed men
filing through. Followed by this one
with the brick-red face who hoisted me up
to look over the fence, all the way to the sea.

COME SPRING

The first warm days of spring, give them to me:
a tepid rain, crocus poking through last year's leaves.

Give me the heart of it: pale yellow, frail blue,
trees bare but for the hard buds, the few birds.

To hear the screen door slam again. To shoo
the flies from the house, the bowled fruit.

I'll take all of it, Mother of Summer, the smell
of manure shoveled over the potatoes. Diesel

fumes from the refuse truck. Scent of creek bottom,
feral, lime laced. Cracked effusion of rotting eggs.

Even sinus infections and rusty rake tines sunk
in rank earth near the shed. Mushroom spores.

The asthmatic crank of winter-bound bikes. Fevers,
flu, cold sores, loose ends. Even the crows,

hawking their dull black cloaks for the shiny wings
of iridescent spring. Let them ride the rippled air

over the barren Sunday parking lots, the farther fields,
where the weeds will grow thorny, wild and tall.

FOR MATTHEW SHEPARD

Here they are again, the bright bugs of June
flittering the evening away, sun stressed
struts holding up the barbed-wire fence, the moon
wandering dangerously, half dark, obsessed,
an abscess spilled into the deep holes snakes
have dug into the spiked hills. What is moot?
The question of love? Figurines on a cake
don't care about gender, stuck on a butte
of icing, Gable y Gable, Garbo
y Garbo, any part an actor can play.
O Shakespeare didn't care if a hobo
wore a dress, a crown, as long as the day
was long, lovely, each word a cut rhinestone,
each touch, kiss, a dab of perfume, cologne.

AFTERLIFE

Even in heaven, when a former waitress goes out
for lunch, she can't help it, can't stop wiping down
the counter, brushing crumbs from the bottoms
of ketchup bottles, cleaning the chunky rim
around the cap with a napkin, tipping big.
Old habits die hard. Old waitresses
die harder, laid out in cheap cardboard coffins
in their lacy blue varicose veins, arches fallen
like grand cathedrals, a row of female Quasimodos:
each finely sprung spine humped from a lifetime
hefting trays. But they have smiles on their faces,
feet up, dancing shoes shined, wispy hair nets
peeled off and tossed in the trash, permed strands
snagged in the knots. You hover over their open caskets
with your fist full of roses and it's their hands
you can't stop staring at. Hands like yours, fingers
scarred, stained, rough, muscles plump
between each knuckle, tough as a man's,
useless now, still as they never were
even at shift's end, gnarled wings folded
between the breasts of faceless women done
with their gossip, their earthly orders,
having poured the day's dark brew
into the last bottomless cup, finished

with mice in the rice bags, roaches
in the walk-in, their eyes sealed shut, deaf
forever to the clatter, the cook, the cries
of the living. Grateful as nuns. Quite dead.

FACE POEM

Your craggy mountain goat face.
Your mole-ridden, whiskered, stumpy fish of a face. Face
I turn to, face I trust, face I trace with grateful fingertips,
jaw like a hinge, washboard forehead, the deep scar a gnarl
along the scritch of your chin.
Your steep, crumbling cliff of a face.
Your U-Haul, bulldozer, crane of a face. Face worthy
of a thousand-dollar bill, a thickly poured, stamped, minted
and excavated coin. Your mile-high billboard of a face looming
up from the pillow of sighs.
Your used car lot of a face, the bumpers
and sprung hoods and headlights of your eyes, your DieHard
battery of a face, the pulpy pith of it, the flare and slur and flange
of your ears, the subterranean up-thrust ridge of your nose.
Your many-planed, light-catching, shadow-etched face.
Your sallow, sun-wracked, jowl-hung face. Eye flash
in flesh folds, gunnel rope and upper lip storm on the high seas
thrash of a face. Your been-there, done-that, anything-goes face.
Luck-of-the-draw fabulous four clubs five knuckled slug
of a face. Toss of the dice face.

LAUNDRY AND CIGARETTES

This tourist ashtray is faux porcelain, creamy white,
gold-plated ridges molded into the four curved corners
where a cigarette can rest. I've counted sixteen
crushed butts, spittle-laced filters of lipsticked
Winstons, half-moon traces the color of dried blood,
to which I've added my own, chemical free,
25 cents a blow American Spirits, waiting
while my laundry tumbles dry in the basement,
stranded for an hour under a 40 watt bulb
amid the drone of machinery, the wet thud
of summer cotton. It's 2004 and I'm tired,
so I poke my lit cigarette into the mess,
herding the butts around the tray.
Under butt #1 The Alamo, its arched doorways
and crumbling adobe, its pitiful American flag,
the paved path landscaped with topiary hedges
clipped into pale green balls. Under butt #2
The Port of Houston, washed-out blue waters
beneath inked-in waves, a cargo ship, the boom
lowering a casket-shaped bale, two palm trees
stuck like shocked weeds near the loading dock.
Butt #3 reveals a row of oil rigs growing
smaller in the nicotine-coated distance.
This section of the tray is labeled *Midland.*

Dead center, a decapitated bull. Longhorn,
of course. Sweeping the ashes aside with a lit coal,
as if painting in reverse, the state flag unfurls
its strict pastures of red, white and blue, its famous,
five-pointed star. Under butt #4 who else
but a buckaroo, one arm held up, face turned away,
no reporters in sight, plaid shirt, bowed legs, corn
yellow hat. Behind him, the lovers on horseback
wearing clean white shirts, collars up, trotting,
heterosexually, through the shadow of Guadalupe Peak.

PUZZLE DUST

When the final piece is lifted and set in place,
completing the field, filling the hole
in a grove of trees, a jagged gap
in the ocean or the flat, black sky.
When the scene is whole before me:
tiny men, arms thin as wicks, walking
briskly along a gray rain-riven street,
the woman bent to her dog under an awning,
his wet head held up with trust,
one white paw in her hand, tip
of his tail I kept trying all day
to press into the starry night, ruffled
hem of her blown-up skirt
that never fit into the distant waves
breaking along the shore,
and the bridge, its rickrack of steel girders
I thought were train tracks or a fallen fence,
when it all, at last, makes sense, a vast
satisfaction fills me: the mossy boulders,
pleasing in their eternal random piles,
the river eased around them, green
with its fever to reach the sea,
a ragged bunch of flowers gathered
from the hills I've locked together,

edge to edge, and placed in a glittering vase
behind a window streaked with rain
which the child in his woolen cap
looks into: boxes of candy wrapped
and displayed, desire burning
in his belly, precursor to the fire
that could have broken his small heart
open like a coal someday
in his future, which for him
is nothing but this empty box
layered with a fine dust, the stuff
from which he was born and will
die into, carried, weightless,
to summer's open door
where I bang my hand against
the cardboard, watch the particles,
like chaff or ashes, vanish in wind.

THE LOST

We all called him Chris, but the night I slept with him
he decided to insist on Christopher. I was the first
to call him, always, by his given name.
He was just one of those back-then boys, one of many
I was determined to possess with that swift, wistful
delirium of the casual romantic. Transient sweetness.
You could say I loved him, the way I loved every boy
I ever slept with, loved them just for being alive,
for being so different from me, for having beards
they shaved so carefully, the blade gliding over
the Adam's apple as it climbed high in their throats,
telling me where to find a cigarette or a pair of socks.
I loved that they had their own private thoughts, thick
blue veins in their necks and cocks, branching veins
I traced up the backs of their calves, their hands
when they hung at their sides. I loved the delicate smells
that rose from the crotches of their jeans,
their crumpled T-shirts. I cherished the nipple-like moles,
the star- and moon-shaped scars. I loved how they came,
quick and hard or slow as a sax solo, rolling away
with a moan, and later how they lingered in the shower,
capturing the water in one hand and splashing it
under an arm. I adored their husky voices and the stories
they told in short bursts or all-night-long installments:

The brother and the bird story. The mother's breast
and the cancer story. I treasured their perfection,
the peach-riven seam that traveled
from the base of their skulls down their long
freckled backs, then disappeared into the darkness,
that when separated, became the morning light
between their legs. I was amazed
by the sheer variety of them, their velocity and vanity,
like carved statues in the rose garden
near the history museum. I studied
the infinite details of difference,
the intimate gesture, the prideful stance.
So when Christopher's boss called me
instead of his twin brother or the mother
who had made him, I was surprised
how simply I got in my car and drove
through traffic like a factory wife,
walked the maze of white hallways
until I found him, and as if I would love him
my whole life, sat without words and held
his unbandaged hand. And I was the one
who returned again to help him begin
to believe it, to unwrap the yellowed gauze,
hold his wrist and look straight at it, then dip

the torn stumps of his fingers into the whirlpool bath,
the saline smell rising like the beginning of a world.
I was surprised by his eyes, each black lash damp, the lids
swollen and open, trusting I could bear the damage.
I saw how he was made of flesh and blood and how
I had to do it. He made me believe I was the only one
who could, the last to have touched him whole.

POOLHALL

For Doralyn

She leans over the felt, her pelvis
grazing the sheened maple rubbed
to a gloss by the musky oils
of men's naked forearms, men
of the rolled-up cuff, the straight shot
and cigarette butt, jeans
with the duff of the workday
still clinging to the knees.
They are in love with the way
she sways and sings to the cuts
on the jukebox, her hair smoke-
scented, her skin washed blue
under the neon Coors sign.
She makes her body a design:
arms crossed, each hand cupping
its own opposite shoulder, thumbs
lifting the straps of her bra, exposing
the deeply etched flesh.
Every weekend is like this:
She gets off work, speeds
to the gas station near
the freeway's edge, changes

in the bathroom, scrubbing
under her arms with the grainy
pink dispenser soap, blotting sweat
and stains with scratchy
brown paper towels.
She trowels on lipstick
in the metal mirror,
her mouth a red blur
in the pale blare of her face,
then she stuffs her apron
into a shopping bag tossed
in the backseat and begins
brushing her long hair down.
And the men are waiting, perched
on the molded barstools
in a quiet row pretending they don't
see her when she walks in. They're
counting toothpicks and quarters,
counting their lucky stars.

IT MUST HAVE BEEN SUMMER

In our neighborhood there were girls,
one with a harelip, one crooked
with polio, another who had a twin
brother, and one who was older
and babysat us all, fed us popcorn
and jelly beans from her cupped hands,
let us choose as many and any color
we wanted while she played LPs
of Sinatra, his felt hat tilted back,
his skinny face tilted toward us.
My father was a pedophile, a word
I didn't yet know, but I knew enough
to do as I was told when she unbuttoned
her shirt and called me her baby.
Just another cul-de-sac girl
who never learned to say no.
We must have made a shabby
Madonna and Child: her cutoff jeans,
sleeveless blouse, my ragged pigtails
and dirt-caked mouth, though no one
would have seen us, her mother
gone to work, her father gone
for good, every curtain closed
in the middle of the afternoon.

It must have been summer,
I was eight or nine, too young
to fathom what she really wanted,
pity and awe colliding with fear,
daring myself to squirm free
and unbolt the door, run home
through the heat, drag my mother
from her cigarettes and beer.
She must have been fifteen
or sixteen, her voice papery,
wide awake and sleepy
at the same time, like the song
Sinatra was singing: "Willow Weep
for Me." She said he made her feel
like she was clipped from velvet.
She meant me no harm, her long hair
sweeping my sun-bruised face,
and all of us damaged anyway.
Then her eyes were half closed
and my hand was half open
and outside her window it was 1960
or '61, the light of California knocking
against the blinds. I never knew anyone
could be sadder than my father

except my mother. The movie houses
were showing *The Misfits, The Hustler,*
A Raisin in the Sun. Bob Dylan
was talking a song in Greenwich Village,
there was trouble in Cuba and Vietnam,
Freedom Riders driving slow
down the streets of Birmingham.
In a few more years I'd have
breasts like hers and men
would be walking on the moon.
Old Blue Eyes crooned to us
through the scratches in the vinyl.
She'd tug her warm milkless nipple
gently from my mouth each time
she got up to turn the record over.

WHAT'S TERRIBLE

It is terrible, but not very terrible.
—Ursula K. Le Guin

To leave your only child waiting at the airport
for an hour, lost in traffic, lost in thought,
is terrible, but not as terrible as kicking
your brother in the stomach, beating your sister
with the phone, forging your mother's name,
spitting on your stepfather's grave.
Though this is less terrible than moving away
to another state without saying good-bye,
just throwing the stereo in the trunk between
the quilts and pillows, strapping the baby
into the backseat and driving off, leaving them all
to their own intricate plots. And though you know
it's wrong to speak of their divorces and minor
car crashes, suicide attempts, evictions,
hospitalizations and Vicodin addictions, their self-
inflicted wounds—the bullet hole in the wall
puttied over with toothpaste—this is not
as terrible as living without them, a dim set
of archetypes in what's left of your memory,
small figurines on the bottom shelf of your
daughter's heart—you've kept her away from them

so she could grow up normal—now stranded
in an airport lounge after a summer with her
born-again father who in spite of you
she demands to see. Terrible thing, the family.
But not so terrible as being abandoned
in a glass room with your suitcase and a bored-
off-her-ass stewardess, flipping through the pages
of a book your mother gave you before you left,
your fractured, frazzled, mysterious mother
who's not sure how to love you, the one
you've forgiven over and over, a book you finally,
in an act of desperation and fear, turn back
to the first torn page and begin, earnestly, to read.

SUPERGLUE

I'd forgotten how fast it happens, the blush of fear
and the feeling of helpless infantile stupidity, stooped
over the sink, warm water gushing into a soapy bowl,
my stuck fingers plunged in, knuckles bumping the glass
like a stillborn pig in formaldehyde, my aging eyes
straining to read the warning label in minus-two type,
lifting the dripping deformed thing up every few seconds
to stare, unbelieving, at the seamless joining, the skin
truly bonded as they say happens *immediately*, thinking:
Truth in Labeling, thinking: This is how I began inside
my mother's belly, before I divided toe from toe, bloomed
into separation like a peach-colored rose, my eyes going slick
and opening, my mouth releasing itself from itself to make
lips, legs one thick fin of thrashing flesh wanting to be two,
unlocking from ankles to knees, cells releasing between
my thighs, not stopping there but wanting more double-ness,
up to the crotch and into the crotch, needing the split
to go deeper, carve a core, a pit, a two-sided womb, with
or without me my body would perform this sideshow
trick and then like a crack in a sidewalk
stop. And I'd carry that want for the rest of my life,
eyes peeled open, mouth agape, the world
piled around me with its visible seams: cheap curtains,
cupboard doors, cut bread on a plate, my husband

appearing in the kitchen on his two strong legs
to see what's wrong, lifting my hand by the wrist
and I want to kiss him, to climb him,
to stuff him inside me and fill that space, poised
on the brink of opening opening opening
as my wrinkled fingers, pale and slippery,
remember themselves, and part.

SISTERS

Grainy ribbons of light
fell through the slats
of the homemade fort
where we lay hip to hip
on the flattened cardboard box,
staring up at nothing.
One of us whistling
over a blade of sharp grass.
Another picking a scab.
Pretending we were beautiful,
pretending we were dead,
listening to our breath, the beast
outside lifting its pale blue
head, its cloudy eye, roaming
the buckling sunlit sidewalks,
calling our shameful names.

A WALK IN THE PARK

Along the Mississippi River
there's a knife-marked bench, a gored
picnic table, familiar things become
flinch worthy, fearfully strange,
like this fly with a thousand eyes
alighting on the exact center of a deeply
carved X. All of it foreign, discordant,
unknown, who is the man loping
into view from behind that
unidentifiable bush, that slinky kid
on a rusty bike, that genderless swag
slogging along the path in baggy pants,
head down, fists swinging like ball-peens?
Is that a chigger on my knee? Isn't that
jogger running this way too fast?
Headlong bird calls collide, wind
bites the trees. Traffic frantic
on the river's freeway side.
This walk in the park is no
walk in the park. Hundreds
of weaponless girls like me
disappear every sky-blue day.

LITTLE MAGNOLIA

Not nearly a woman like the backyard cedar
whose branches fall and curl,
whose curved body sways in wind,
the little magnolia is still a girl,
her first blossoms tied like white strips of rag
to the tips of her twiggy pigtails.

Who are the trees? They live
half in air, half below ground,

both rooted and homeless, like the man
who wedges his life between
the windbreak wall of the Laundromat
and the broken fence, a strip of gritty earth
where he's unfolded his section
of clean cardboard, his Goodwill blanket.
Here's his cup, his candle, his knife.

GIRL CHILD

Shouldn't she be in bed, you think,
as she slaps her hands on the rocks
of your bare knees, climbs you like
a fence, one sweaty palm the size
of a pocket watch, warm, a little
sticky, pressed to your cheek.
It's painful to look into her face,
this strange child touching you
as if she knows you and trusts you,
sent here to say whatever
hardened you all those years ago
was not your fault, though when you
look into her eyes you see how it was,
how it will always be, someone
touching her back.

THE IDEA OF HOUSEWORK

What good does it do anyone
to have a drawer full of clean knives,
the tines of tiny pitchforks
gleaming in plastic bins, your face
reflected eight times over
in the oval bowls of spoons?
What does it matter that the doormat
is swept clear of leaves, high corners
broomed of spiderwebs, blankets
shaken so sleep's duff and fuzz,
dead skin flakes, lost strands of hair,
flicker down on the newly cut grass?
Who cares if bread crumbs collect
on the countertop, if photographs
of the ones you love go gray with dust,
if milk jugs pile up, unreturned,
on the back porch near the old dog's dish?
Oh to rub the windows with vinegar,
the trees behind them revealing
their sap-streaked leaves. Oh the bleachy,
waxy, soapy perfume of spring.
Why should the things of this world
shine so? Tell me if you know.

MUSIC IN THE MORNING

When I think of the years he drank,
the scars on his chin, his thinning hair,
the eye that still weeps decades
after the blow, my knees weaken
with gratitude for whatever
kept him safe, whatever stopped
the glass from shattering, sheering
something vital, the fist from lowering,
exploding an artery, pressing
a blood clot toward the back of his brain.
Now he sits calmly on the couch, reading,
refusing to wear the glasses
I bought him, holding the open book
at arm's length from his chest.
Behind him the windows are smoky with mist
and the tile floor is pushing its night chill
up through the bare soles of his feet.
I like to think he survived
in order to find me, in order to arrive here
sober, tired from a long night. Music
on the radio. Coffee. So he could look up
and see me, standing in the kitchen
in his torn T-shirt, its frayed hem
brushing my knees. But I know it's only luck

that delivered him here, luck and a love
that had nothing to do with me. Except
that this is what we sometimes get
if we live long enough. If we are patient
with our lives.

KISSING AGAIN

Kissing again, after a long drought of
not kissing—too many kids, bills, windows

needing repair. Sex, yes, though squeezed in
between the minor depths of anger, despair—

standing up amid the laundry
or fumbling onto the strip of rug between

the coffee table and the couch. Quick, furtive,
like birds. A dance on the wing, but no time

for kissing, the luxuriant tonguing of another
spongy tongue, the deft flicking and feral sucking,

that prolonged lapping that makes a smooth stone
of the brain. To be lost in it, your body tumbled

in sea waves, no up or down, just salt
and the liquid swells set in motion

by the moon, by a tremor in Istanbul, the waft
of a moth wing before it plows into a halo of light.

Praise the deep lustrous kiss that lasts minutes,
blossoms into what feels like days, fields of tulips

glossy with dew, low purple clouds piling in
beneath the distant arch of a bridge. One

after another they storm your lips, each kiss
a caress, autonomous and alive, spilling

into each other, streams into creeks into rivers
that grunt and break upon the gorge. Let the tongue,

in its wisdom, release its stores, let the mouth,
tired of talking, relax into its shapes of give

and receive, its plush swelling, its slick
round reveling, its primal reminiscence

that knows only the one robust world.

SAVAGES

Those two shelves, down there.
—Adrienne Rich

For Matthew, Mike, Michael and Carl

They buy poetry like gang members
buy guns—for aperture, caliber,
heft and defense. They sit on the floor
in the stacks, thumbing through Keats
and Plath, Levine and Olds, four boys
in a bookstore, black glasses, brackish hair,
rumpled shirts from the bin at St. Vincent de Paul.
One slides a warped hardback
from the bottom shelf, the others
scoot over to check the dates,
the yellowed sheaves ride smooth
under their fingers.
One reads a stanza in a whisper,
another turns the page, and their heads
almost touch, temple to temple—toughs
in a huddle, barbarians before a hunt, kids
hiding in an alley while sirens spiral by.
When they finish reading one closes
the musty cover like the door

on Tutankhamen's tomb. They are savage
for knowledge, for beauty and truth.
They crawl on their knees to find it.

AGAINST ENDINGS

On the street outside the window
someone is talking to someone else,

a baffling song, no words, only the music

of voices—low contralto of questions,
laughter's plucked strings—voices in darkness

below stars where someone straddles a bike
up on the balls of his feet, and someone else

stands firm on a curb, her arms crossed, two

dogs nearby listening to the human duet,
stars falling through a summer night

a sudden car passing, rap song thumping,

but the voices, unhurried, return, obligatos afloat
on the humid air, tiny votives wavering

as porch lights go out—not wanting it to stop—

and Mars rising over the flower shop, up
through the telephone wires

TONIGHT I AM IN LOVE

Tonight, I am in love with poetry,
with the good words that saved me,
with the men and women who
uncapped their pens and laid the ink
on the blank canvas of the page.

I am shameless in my love; their faces
rising on the smoke and dust at the end
of day, their sullen eyes and crusty hearts,
the murky serum now turned to chalk
along the gone cords of their spines.

I'm reciting the first anonymous lines
that broke night's thin shell: *sonne under wode.*
A baby is born us bliss to bring. I have labored
sore and suffered death. Jesus' wounds so wide.

I am wounded with tenderness for all who labored
in dim rooms with their handful of words,
battering their full hearts against the moon.

They flee from me that sometime did me seek.
Wake, now my love, awake: for it is time.
For God's sake hold your tongue and let me love!

What can I do but love them? Sore throated
they call from beneath blankets of grass,
through the wind-torn elms, near the river's
edge, voices shorn of everything but the one
hope, the last question, the first loss, calling

Slow, slow, fresh fount, keep time with my salt tears.
Whenas in silks my Julia goes, calling *Why do I*
 languish thus, drooping and dull as if I were all earth?

Now they are bones, the sweet ones who once
considered a cat, a nightingale, a hare, a lamb,
a fly, who saw a Tyger burning, who passed
five summers and five long winters, passed them
and saved them and gave them away in poems.

They could not have known how I would love them,
worlds fallen from their mortal fingers.
When I cannot see to read or walk alone
along the slough, I will hear you, I will
bring the longing in your voices to rest
against my old, tired heart and call you back.

CELLO

When a dead tree falls in a forest
it often falls into the arms
of a living tree. The dead,
thus embraced, rasp in wind,
slowly carving a niche
in the living branch, shearing away
the rough outer flesh, revealing
the pinkish, yellowish, feverish
inner bark. For years
the dead tree rubs its fallen body
against the living, building
its dead music, making its raw mark,
wearing the tough bough down
as it moans and bends, the deep
rosined bow sound of the living
shouldering the dead.

September 10, 2002

THE BIRTHDAY PARTY

For Ehud

We're in his backyard again, as we have been each July 17th,
the pop of fireworks fading, finally, and instead of those brief
distant flowers of light we watch his face lower over
the wavering candles, how many now? We've come again
to his door, bags in our hands, hastily wrapped gift,
banana bread, a cold bottle, some story we've been saving
that might make him laugh. We can hope
he'll last out the year, his face ashen, the gray
of the oncoming winter, the daily chemo treatments
now down to one a week, then one a month, when again
the color will flood back into his face. It's happened before,
he's come back from death, resurrected so many times now.
He takes his small son onto his skinny lap and together
they blow the candles out, open the gifts, the heavy hardback
he can hardly hold up, the Kurosawa video trilogy, jumble
of homegrown vegetables, a New York Yankees "away" jersey.
He's cold now and so he tugs it on and the gray looks
good on him, hangs rakishly from his shoulders
so that he seems suddenly boyish, as if he could really
see a baseball and hit it. The yellow jackets feeding
on the cake's drizzled icing force us inside to stand
under the harsh kitchen lights, then into the living room

where we break up into small groups, his older son, 14,
talking about his first job as if his father weren't close
to dying. A job in a movie house, not a big blockbuster
but a renovated theater with crushed velour seats,
a patched screen, one that shows the kind of films you need
an attention span to watch.

ONE CELL

. . . contains a digitally coded database larger, in information content, than all 30 volumes of the Encyclopedia Britannica *put together.*
—Richard Dawkins, from *The Blind Watchmaker*

So in our beds or in the beds of lovers,
when we leave we leave volumes
of information, the book of our days
lost to ourselves, sloughed off into the world.
As we wander a filthy city street
we grow new cells, pungent with the old codes,
so we can stop walking, remember
the day we wept openly for a man
in a casket, the night we touched a glass
to our lips and saw all creation
in a stranger's face. The pain of childbirth
comes back, the scent of magnolia, a song
from a commercial, an afternoon carnival,
a choir. Our cells retain it, pinhead
sponges soaking up whatever we need
to keep walking, to keep stumbling into
the blinding darkness ahead.

MORNING SONG

This morning begins almost purely, coffee
enveloped in cream, those clouds that bloom up
like madness in a cup, and I take the first swallow
before the color changes, taste the bitterness
and the faint sweet behind it, steam
rubbing my nose, an animal nuzzle,
and the sharp, nearly painful heat
at the back of my tongue, the liquid
unraveling down the raw tunnel of my throat.

And I feel my body fully, vessel of desire,
my stomach a pond of want and warmth,
utterly human, divine and awake. And I can hear
each bird's separate song, the *chirt* and *scree*,
the *sip, sip, sip*, the dwindle and uplift yearning,
the *soup's on, soup's on, let up, let it go*
of each individual voice, and I know I am here,
in this widening light, as we all are, with them,
even the most damaged among us or lonely
or nearly dead, and that for each of us there is
some small sound like an unseen bird or
a red bike grinding along the gravel path
that could wake us, and take us home.

This morning I think I'm prepared for
the final diminishment, with something
like a waking, ready awe. My complaints
folded and put away in a drawer
like needlework, unfinished, intricate
woven roads that go nowhere or disappear
in the distance, rough wanderings
that have brought me here, to this
sleep-repaired morning, these singing trees
and into my own listening body.

STARLING

Tail a fanfare and the devil's
kindling. Oh to be a rider
on that purple storm. Not
peacock or eagle but lowly
starling, Satan's bird,
spreading her spotted wings
over the Valley of Bones.
To build a home within her, stark
shanty for the soul, bonfire stoked
with pine-sap sage, smoke
rising through her ribs, her skin,
tainting the undersides of leaves.
Marrow house from which the one
wild word escapes. Stave and barrel
world of want. Of late, my plush
black nest. My silver claw
and gravel craw. My only song.

ACKNOWLEDGMENTS

Grateful acknowledgment is made to the following publications where these poems or earlier versions of them first appeared:

The Alaska Quarterly Review: "Laundry and Cigarettes"
The American Poetry Review: "The Crossing," "Morning Song," "The Life of Trees," "Poolhall," "What's Terrible," "Face Poem," "Superglue"
ART/LIFE: "Against Endings"
Barrow Street: "Democracy"
Burnside Review: "My Brother's Grave"
Cairn: "Hummingbird," "Sisters," "Moon in the Window"
The Canary River Review: "What's Broken"
Calapooya: "One Cell"
Court Green: "The Lost," "For Matthew Shepard"
Great River Review: "Little Magnolia," "Puzzle Dust"
Harvard Review: "Music in the Morning"
Ms. magazine: "The Germans"
Naked Knuckle: "A Walk in the Park"
Passaic Literary Review: "It Must Have Been Summer"
Quercus Review: "Cello," "The Idea of Housework," "Her First," "Afterlife"
Shenandoah: "Vacation Sex"

Solo: "Tonight I Am in Love"
The Southeast Review: "The Last Days of Pompeii"
Speakeasy: "Come Spring," "Facts about the Moon"
ZYZZYVA: "Kissing Again"

"The Idea of Housework" was reprinted in *Sweeping Beauty: Contemporary Women Poets on Housework*, University of Iowa Press. "Cello" was originally published in *Poets Against the War*, Nation Books, and was reprinted in *Oregon Poets Against the War*, Rainy Nights Press. "Facts about the Moon" was reprinted in *The Blue Fifth Review*, online. "Hummingbird" was published as a broadside by Red Dragonfly Press.

Thank you to my comrades Joseph Millar, Phil and Fran Levine, Sharon Olds, Marie Howe, Jane Hirshfield, Frank Gaspar, Joel Rosen, Maxine Scates and Bill Cadbury, Kim Addonizio, Ellen Bass, Marjorie Sandor and Tracy Daugherty, Ginger Andrews, Doug Anderson, David Bradley, Karen Ford and Donald Laird, my boys, Matthew Dickman, Michael Dickman, Mike McGriff, and my girl, Tristem.

Special thanks to Geri Digiorno and the Petaluma Poetry Walk, the Grubin Family for their Poet's Sanctuary on the 14th Floor in New York City, and to Carol Houck Smith for her patience and faith.

Gratitude also to Caldera in Sisters, Oregon, the Banff

Center for the Arts in Alberta, Canada, and the Anderson Center for the Arts where many of these poems were written, and for the support of the John Simon Guggenheim Foundation and the National Endowment for the Arts.

—

And finally, in memory of Judy Stedman, Reetika Vazarani, and Jehan Komunyakaa

ABOUT THE AUTHOR

Dorianne Laux is the author of three previous collections of poetry. She is also coauthor, with Kim Addonizio, of *The Poet's Companion: A Guide to the Pleasures of Writing Poetry* (W. W. Norton, 1997). Her work has appeared in *The Best American Poetry, The American Poetry Review, Shenandoah, Ms.* magazine, *Ploughshares, Barrow Street,* and *Five Points.* Among her awards are a Pushcart Prize for poetry, two fellowships from the National Endowment for the Arts, and a Guggenheim Fellowship. Laux is an associate professor and works in the University of Oregon's Creative Writing Program. She lives in Eugene, Oregon, with her husband, poet Joseph Millar, and her daughter, Tristem.